Outside My Window

Addison C. Marley

Fulton Books, Inc.
Meadville, PA

Published by Fulton Books 2021

ISBN 978-1-63710-964-9 (hardcover)
ISBN 978-1-63710-963-2 (digital)

Printed in the United States of America

To my granddaughter Addison who spent her first Christmas on the PICU floor of Vanderbilt's Children's Hospital at just four months old. She inspired the writing of this book.

To my twin boys who were born six weeks premature and were in Kosair's Children's Hospital.

To all the children who, for whatever reason, are unable to go outside and play due to an illness.

And finally to my daughter, who has always been there for me.

This book is meant as one of hope that someday we will all play outside our window.

Addison C. Marley

Illustrations by: Jasmine Smith

Outside my window, the birds flying by...

Stretching their wings way up in the sky.

Outside my window,
there are squirrels in the trees...

Watching and waiting
to come and play with me.

8

Someday when I can,
I'm going to be...

Outside my window
as happy as can be.

Someday when I can,
I'm going to play...

Outside my window
every day!

Outside my window,
the Sun is shining bright...

14

Watching over my friends,
from morning till night.

Outside my window, my friends wave to me...

Hoping that one day, outside's where I'll be.

Someday when I can,
I'm going to be...

Outside my window
as happy as can be.

Someday when I can,
I'm going to play...

Outside my window
every day!

24

WHAT DO YOU SEE OUTSIDE YOUR WINDOW?

About the Author

Addison C. Marley is the father of three kids and "Gdaddy" to three granddaughters—Addison, Anabelle, and Cleo. In this, his first published children's book, he hopes to reach out to the children who, for whatever reason, are unable to play outside and bring them a hope that one day they too will be able to. Having raised twin boys who were born premature, who spent several weeks in Kosair's Children's Hospital, and later struggled with breathing problems, Addison C. Marley knows all too well the difficulties of seeing a child wanting to go outside and play but is unable due to illnesses. This book, *Outside My Window*, was first penned when Addison C. Marley's granddaughter was just four months old and found herself spending her first Christmas in Monroe Carell Jr. Children's Hospital in Nashville, Tennessee, in the Pediatric Intensive Care Unit. The author hopes that the words and illustrations in this book find their way into the hearts of children and bring them hope. Addison C. Marley grew up in Princeton, Kentucky, and now resides in Eddyville, Kentucky.

CPSIA information can be obtained
at www.ICGtesting.com
Printed in the USA
LVHW050228071221
705458LV00002B/8